AF413586

THE SYMPHONY OF THE SOUL

EXPLORING VISUAL, MUSICAL, AND PERFORMANCE ARTS IN THERAPEUTIC HARMONY

DR. MINAKSHI BANSAL

Copyright © Dr. Minakshi Bansal
All Rights Reserved.

This book has been self-published with all reasonable efforts taken to make the material error-free by the author. No part of this book shall be used, reproduced in any manner whatsoever without written permission from the author, except in the case of brief quotations embodied in critical articles and reviews.

The Author of this book is solely responsible and liable for its content including but not limited to the views, representations, descriptions, statements, information, opinions and references ["Content"]. The Content of this book shall not constitute or be construed or deemed to reflect the opinion or expression of the Publisher or Editor. Neither the Publisher nor Editor endorse or approve the Content of this book or guarantee the reliability, accuracy or completeness of the Content published herein and do not make any representations or warranties of any kind, express or implied, including but not limited to the implied warranties of merchantability, fitness for a particular purpose. The Publisher and Editor shall not be liable whatsoever for any errors, omissions, whether such errors or omissions result from negligence, accident, or any other cause or claims for loss or damages of any kind, including without limitation, indirect or consequential loss or damage arising out of use, inability to use, or about the reliability, accuracy or sufficiency of the information contained in this book.

Made with ♥ on the Notion Press Platform
www.notionpress.com

DEDICATION

This book is dedicated to all who find solace and strength in the arts, to the healers who guide through the power of creative expression, and to every soul that has ever been touched by the transformative beauty of a note, a brushstroke, or a dance move. May this work inspire you to continue exploring the deep connection between art and healing, and to embrace the boundless possibilities that creativity holds for enriching human lives.

ԲԲԲ

Contents

Contents

Contents

Prayer

"Om Bhadram Karnebhih Shrinuyama Devah
Bhadram Pashyemakshabhiryajatrah
Sthirairangais Tushtuvamsastanubhih
Vyashema Devahitam Yadayuh
Svasti Na Indro Vriddhashravah
Svasti Nah Pusha Vishwavedah
Svasti Nastarkshyo Arishtanemih
Svasti No Brihaspatir Dadhatu
Om Shantih Shantih Shantih"

This mantra is a prayer for universal well-being, invoking the blessings of various deities for protection, health, and happiness. It emphasizes the importance of experiencing the auspicious through all senses and living a life aligned with divine purpose. The repetition of "Shantih" at the end signifies a deep desire for peace in the individual, the environment, and the universe at large. This mantra is often recited as a prayer for peace, prosperity, and the physical and spiritual well-being of all beings.

ᗞᗞᗞ

About The Author

Dr. Minakshi Bansal, born in the bustling metropolis of Delhi, India, has led a life steeped in artistry, scholarly pursuit, and an unwavering commitment to societal betterment. Following her marriage, she relocated to Ahmedabad, Gujarat, where she has since blossomed into a multifaceted beacon of inspiration for many. Dr. Minakshi is not only recognized as a gifted artist in the realm of Fine Arts but also as an esteemed author, a devoted social worker and a dedicated research scholar in Psychology. Her journey, marked by a profound dedication to elevating those around her, especially the downtrodden and underprivileged children of society, is a testament to her deep-seated belief in the transformative power of engagement and empathy.

From her earliest days, Minakshi was distinguished by an insatiable appetite for reading. Her literary universe was inhabited by characters and narratives that spanned ethical tales, motivational and inspirational stories, and the mythic parables imbued with life lessons. This voracious reading habit was not merely for personal edification but was driven by a desire to distill and disseminate the essence of these narratives to foster the development of students and peers alike. She was particularly captivated by the lives and teachings of historical figures and spiritual leaders such as Adi Shankaracharya, Swami Vivekananda, Dr. APJ Abdul Kalam, Mahamana Pandit Madan Mohan Malviya, Mahatma Gandhi, Sardar Vallabhai Patel, and Vinoba Bhave, among others. Their philosophies and life stories fueled her ambition to embody their ideals of resilience, selflessness, and relentless pursuit of knowledge.

Dr. Minakshi's academic and practical engagement with psychology has been equally noteworthy. As a research scholar, her focus has been on exploring the intricate tapestry of the human psyche, aiming to unlock the potential for psychological well-being and societal harmony. Her scholarly work is complemented by her active involvement in social work, where she employs her academic insights to make tangible differences in the lives of the underprivileged. Her endeavours in social work are characterized by an innovative approach that combines traditional wisdom with contemporary psychological practices to address the multifaceted challenges faced by these communities.

Her artistic talents, another facet of her diverse capabilities, are not merely a personal passion but also serve as a medium through which she communicates and connects with others. Her art, rich in symbolism and emotional depth, reflects her philosophical inquiries and social concerns, offering viewers a glimpse into the breadth of her intellect and the depth of her compassion.

In addition to her contributions to the arts and social sciences, Dr. Minakshi has embraced the healing arts of Pranic Healing, mastering the techniques developed by Master Choa Kok Sui. This practice, which focuses on the manipulation of Prana or life energy to heal the body and aura, has been both a personal journey of discovery and a means through which she extends her healing touch to others. Her proficiency in Pranic Healing is complemented by her advocacy and teaching of various forms of meditation aimed at rejuvenation, personal betterment, and the cultivation of harmony within individuals and communities alike.

Dr. Minakshi's life is a narrative of relentless pursuit, not just of personal achievement but of the upliftment and empowerment of society at large. Her diverse interests and talents—spanning the arts, literature, psychology, and the healing practices—converge on a singular path of service. She embodies the spirit of the luminaries who inspired her, channelling their legacy through her actions and teachings. Through her books, art, and social initiatives, she continues to inspire a new generation to embark on their own journeys of self-discovery, resilience, and altruism.

Her commitment to social betterment, particularly her focus on uplifting underprivileged children, reflects a deep understanding of the transformative potential of education and personal development. By integrating her knowledge of psychology, her artistic sensibilities, and her healing practices, Dr. Bansal has developed a holistic approach to social work that addresses both the immediate needs and the long-term well-being of the communities she serves.

As an author, Dr. Minakshi's writings offer a blend of inspirational insights, practical wisdom, and reflective contemplations drawn from her extensive reading and life experiences. Her books serve as a guide for those seeking to navigate the complexities of life with grace, resilience, and purpose. Through her narratives, she extends an invitation to her readers to explore the depths of their own potential and to contribute meaningfully to the collective well-being of society.

In Dr. Minakshi Bansal, we find a remarkable synthesis of the artist, the scholar, the healer, and the social activist. Her life's work stands as a beacon of hope and a source of inspiration for individuals seeking to make a difference in the world. Her story is a compelling reminder of the power of individual action, rooted in compassion and driven by a profound commitment to the betterment of humanity. Dr. Minakshi's legacy is not just in the tangible outcomes of her efforts but in the enduring spirit of inquiry, empathy, and service that she embodies.

Preface

In this exploration of the interconnections between art and therapy, we delve into the profound ways in which the visual, musical, and performance arts contribute not just to individual healing but also to societal well-being. The arts have long been a refuge, a place of comfort and expression, for souls seeking solace and understanding. This book examines how these artistic disciplines, often celebrated for their aesthetic value, hold deep therapeutic potential and are increasingly recognized as vital tools in psychological healing and emotional development.

At the heart of this exploration is the belief that art has the unique ability to communicate the incommunicable, to express what words cannot, and to reach deep into the human psyche to effect transformation and healing. Art transcends cultural and linguistic barriers, creating a universal language that speaks to the human condition in all its diversity. Through the lens of therapy, art becomes more than an expression—it becomes a dialogue, one spoken in the silent languages of brushstrokes, musical notes, and bodily movements.

As we navigate the chapters of this journey, we encounter the visual arts—painting, sculpture, and photography—each offering its unique form of reflection and expression. These arts allow individuals to project their inner experiences onto canvas, clay, or film, transforming abstract emotions into tangible forms that can be observed, analyzed, and understood. The process of creating art is as cathartic as it is revealing, providing both a mirror and a map to parts of ourselves that we might otherwise struggle to access.

Music, with its rhythms and harmonies, affects us at our core, resonating with our primal instincts and evoking a spectrum of emotions from joy to sorrow, tranquility to agitation. It is both a reflection of cultural heritage and a personal experience deeply rooted in the moment of its creation or performance. Music therapy harnesses these qualities, employing melodies and harmonies to soothe, stimulate, and sometimes confront the psychological and emotional issues that individuals face.

Performance arts, encompassing dance and theater, offer a dynamic and powerful medium for therapy. These arts involve the body as much as the mind, promoting physical wellness alongside emotional and psychological healing. Dance therapy, for instance, uses movement to help individuals express emotions that they cannot articulate, while drama therapy allows individuals to explore new identities, rehearse desired outcomes, and gain mastery over their narratives through role-play.

Each form of art offers a unique pathway to healing, yet all share common threads. They provide an outlet for expression, serve as tools for communication, and act as instruments of change. The therapeutic settings in which these arts are applied are as varied as the techniques themselves, ranging from clinical environments to community centers and schools. In each setting, the primary goal remains the same: to harness the transformative power of art to improve lives.

The integration of art into therapeutic practices is not merely about adapting artistic techniques for clinical use; it is about redefining what it means to heal and be healed. It challenges traditional notions of medicine and therapy, proposing a more holistic approach to health—one that recognizes the importance of the mind-body connection and the profound impact of aesthetic and sensory experiences on our overall well-being.

As we look forward to the future of art therapy, it is clear that the field is ripe for innovation. Digital technologies, new media, and interdisciplinary approaches open up exciting possibilities for the expansion and deeper integration of arts into therapeutic practices. These developments promise to make art therapy more accessible, allowing it to reach a broader audience and address a wider range of needs.

However, as we embrace these advancements, we must also remain mindful of the intrinsic value of the human touch—the irreplaceable quality of personal interaction and the profound connection that occurs when individuals share a physical space and a moment in time. Whether through a brushstroke, a dance move, or a musical note, the essence of art therapy lies in its ability to foster connections—between the self and others, the individual and the community, the personal and the universal.

This book is an invitation to view the arts through a therapeutic lens, to see beyond their beauty and delve into their potential to heal and transform. It is a tribute to the artists, therapists, and individuals who have experienced and facilitated this transformation, and a testament to the enduring power of art to speak directly to the soul. As you journey through these pages, may you find not only information and insight but also inspiration and a renewed sense of wonder at the complex symphony of the human spirit.

Dr. Minakshi Bansal
Social Activist
Ahmedabad, Gujarat, Bharat

ॐॐॐ

ONE

The Canvas of Emotions: Understanding Art Therapy

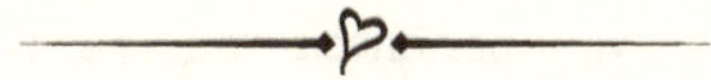

Art therapy stands at the crossroads of creative expression and psychological healing, serving as a transformative tool for individuals seeking to uncover, explore, and resolve deep-seated emotions. It is founded on the belief that artistic expression can facilitate communication, foster emotional growth, and aid in the recovery from a variety of mental health issues. This unique therapeutic approach utilizes various forms of visual art—including painting, drawing, sculpture, and other media—as a means of expressing thoughts and feelings that are otherwise difficult to articulate.

The practice of art therapy is grounded in the idea that the creative process involved in artistic self-expression helps people to resolve conflicts and problems, develop interpersonal skills, manage behavior, reduce stress, increase self-esteem and self-awareness, and achieve insight. It offers a non-verbal outlet and cognitive distraction from distress, allowing individuals to explore their emotions in a space that is free from the constraints of words.

One of the core principles of art therapy is its focus on the process of creation rather than the final product. This process-oriented approach allows individuals to engage in self-exploration through the manipulation of art materials, which in turn facilitates a journey inward. The act of making art is therapeutic in itself as it can be a meditative and introspective practice that helps individuals connect with their inner selves. It provides a safe environment where emotions can be expressed and examined without judgment or social inhibition.

Art therapy can be particularly effective for those who find it hard to express their feelings verbally. This might include children, who may not have the vocabulary to fully express complex emotions, or individuals who have experienced trauma and find it difficult to speak about their experiences directly. Through the use of symbols and imagery, art therapy allows for the externalization of that which is internal, making tangible the intangible aspects of one's psychological experience.

Moreover, art therapy is not confined to any specific demographic or psychological condition. It is used across a broad spectrum of settings, including hospitals, wellness centers, schools, rehabilitation facilities, and private practices. Within these settings, art therapists work with a diverse range of individuals, including those suffering from anxiety, depression, PTSD, chronic illness, addiction, and social and emotional difficulties among others.

In clinical practice, art therapists are trained to recognize the nonverbal symbols and metaphors that are often expressed through the art process, which might be overlooked by other therapy types. This can be particularly vital in identifying issues and emotions that the client may not yet be ready to verbalize. The art therapist guides the individual through the process of creating art and helps to elucidate the meanings, connotations, and implications of their art, thus providing valuable insights into the individual's personal situation.

Furthermore, the flexible nature of art as therapy allows it to be tailored to the individual's needs. For instance, in group settings, art therapy can foster a sense of community and shared experience among participants, providing social support and reducing feelings of isolation. On the other hand, in a more private setting, it can be a deeply personal experience that promotes individual growth and self-discovery.

As the field of art therapy continues to grow, its applications are expanding beyond traditional mental health environments to include settings such as corporate offices, education systems, and community centers, where it is used to enhance overall well-being and creativity. This expansion reflects a growing recognition of the benefits of a holistic approach to health and wellness—one that includes the mind, body, and spirit.

Art therapy offers a unique and powerful means of communication, healing, and expression for individuals across all stages of life. It underscores the profound impact that the arts can have on our emotional well-being and highlights the creativity inherent in the human spirit. As more people turn to art therapy to face their psychological challenges, it remains a beacon of hope and a testament to the transformative power of art.

ppp

"Art speaks where words fail, painting emotions in strokes of color that words could never capture, creating a silent symphony that resonates within the deepest parts of our soul."

ᗡᗡᗡ

TWO

Harmony and Health: The Healing Power of Music

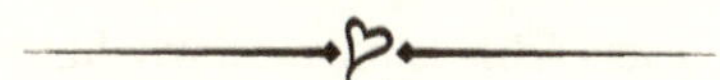

Music has long been recognized as a powerful medium capable of influencing human emotions and behaviors. Its therapeutic applications are vast, offering benefits that span physical, emotional, and cognitive domains. Music therapy, an established health profession, leverages the intrinsic qualities of music to address the specific therapeutic needs of individuals, fostering healing and promoting overall well-being.

The roots of music therapy can be traced back to ancient civilizations where music was an integral part of daily life and rituals, often used for its healing properties. In contemporary settings, music therapy has evolved into a structured practice that utilizes musical interventions to achieve individualized goals within a therapeutic relationship by a credentialed professional. The interventions might include creating, singing, moving to, and/ or listening to music, depending on the specific needs of the client.

One of the fundamental ways music therapy aids individuals is through its capacity to manage stress. Stress reduction is achieved through the soothing properties of music, which can significantly lower cortisol levels, a hormone associated with stress. Listening to calming music has been shown to decrease heart rate and blood pressure, physiological responses that are often elevated during stress.

This calming effect not only helps to reduce anxiety but also aids individuals in coping with stress-related health issues such as heart disease and mental health disorders.

Music therapy is particularly effective in pain management. Studies have demonstrated that music can distract from pain and discomfort, serve as a form of meditation, and even alter the perception of pain levels. This is particularly beneficial in hospitals where patients undergoing surgery or those in chronic pain have found relief through music therapy sessions. The mechanism behind this involves music's ability to trigger the release of endorphins, the body's natural painkillers.

In the realm of mental health, music therapy offers significant benefits for people suffering from mood disorders such as depression and anxiety. It provides an outlet for expression, particularly for those who find it difficult to express their feelings verbally. For instance, playing an instrument can serve as a form of expression for complex emotions, while singing can help improve mood and boost confidence.

Music therapy also promotes mindfulness and presence, helping individuals to focus on the present moment and alleviate symptoms of anxiety.

The benefits of music therapy extend to cognitive functions as well.

It has been particularly noted for its effect on brain regions involved in concentration, attention, and memory. For patients with neurodegenerative disorders such as Alzheimer's and dementia, music therapy can be used to recall memories, reduce agitation, and enhance communication and motor skills.

Even in individuals without cognitive impairments, music can improve concentration and memory performance by providing a rhythmic and melodic structure that helps organize cognitive output.

In addition to mental health and cognitive improvements, music therapy provides substantial benefits in the context of physical rehabilitation. For patients recovering from stroke or traumatic brain injuries, music therapy has been used to facilitate movement and coordination.

Music's rhythmic components can help in the synchronization of movement, which is beneficial in physical therapy to improve gait and muscle control.

For children and adolescents, music therapy serves as a unique tool for social development and educational enhancement. It helps in developing communication skills and social interaction. In educational settings, music can facilitate learning and retention of information through songs and rhythms that enhance auditory development and memory.

Furthermore, music therapy has been found to have a unique impact on the emotional and psychological development of individuals. It helps in building resilience, enhancing self-awareness, and promoting emotional expression.

The interactive nature of music therapy, involving the music therapist and client, also helps in building trust and improving interpersonal relationships.

In summary, music therapy offers a multifaceted therapeutic approach that impacts various aspects of health and well-being. Its broad applicability and effectiveness make it a valuable tool in therapeutic settings, capable of addressing a wide range of physical, emotional, and cognitive issues.

As research continues to evolve, the scope of music therapy is likely to expand, continuing to unlock the profound and myriad effects of music on human health and wellness.

♪♪♪

"In the rhythm of music, we find the unspoken
truths of our hearts, each note a stepping stone on
the path to emotional clarity and healing."

♡♡♡

THREE

MOVEMENT AS MEDICINE: THE ROLE OF DANCE IN MENTAL WELLNESS

Dance therapy, recognized formally as dance/movement therapy (DMT), embodies the psychological and physical union that occurs when motion and emotion converge. Rooted in the idea that body and mind are inseparable, dance therapy is built on the premise that changes in movement can reflect, and even affect, one's mental and emotional state. As a discipline within the arts therapies, it harnesses the natural movement of the body as a therapeutic tool to promote emotional, cognitive, physical, and social integration of individuals.

At its core, dance therapy is predicated on the concept of body-mind connectivity, suggesting that the way we move can influence how we think and feel. It operates on the principle that when people allow their bodies to move freely, they can tap into deep-seated emotions and memories that might be difficult to access through verbal communication alone. This form of therapy is particularly potent for individuals who are distanced from their emotions or who find verbal expression challenging.

The therapeutic use of dance has been effectively implemented across various populations and settings, ranging from hospitals and rehabilitation centers to schools and private practices. It has shown remarkable efficacy in treating individuals with developmental, medical, social, physical, and psychological impairments. Dance therapy utilizes movement to help individuals achieve a greater sense of body awareness, self-esteem, and self-expression; to improve their mental and physical health; and to enhance their quality of life.

One of the primary areas where dance therapy has shown significant benefits is in the management of stress and anxiety. The physical act of dancing releases endorphins, the body's natural mood lifters, which can decrease the perception of pain and generate a state of well-being. Furthermore, the rhythmic nature of dance provides a means of relaxation and stress relief that is both dynamic and soothing. For individuals dealing with anxiety, dance therapy offers a structured outlet for the physical symptoms of stress, while simultaneously allowing for the expression of pent-up emotions, aiding in the alleviation of anxiety symptoms.

In the context of depression, dance therapy has been utilized as a powerful tool to combat the inertia that often accompanies mood disorders. By engaging in dance, individuals may feel more energized and motivated, which can be particularly beneficial for those experiencing the lethargy associated with depression. The expressive aspect of dance allows individuals to convey their feelings in a physical manner, which can help to lighten the burden of emotional distress. Moreover, the social aspect of dance—in groups or therapeutic settings—provides a sense of connection and community, which is crucial for individuals feeling isolated by their depression.

Dance therapy also plays a significant role in the cognitive and emotional development of children and adolescents. Through dance, young individuals learn about communication, turn-taking, and emotional regulation. These skills are vital as they navigate their early developmental stages. Dance activities that require remembering routines can enhance memory, attention, and concentration, while improvised dance can boost creativity and problem-solving skills.

For older adults, dance therapy can contribute significantly to cognitive preservation and physical health. It can help in maintaining and improving range of motion, balance, and coordination, which are essential for preventing falls and promoting physical confidence. Furthermore, dance can also serve as a cognitive exercise, helping to keep the brain active and engaged, which is vital in slowing the progression of cognitive decline associated with aging.

Dance therapy extends its benefits to those with chronic health conditions as well, including Parkinson's disease and multiple sclerosis, where it improves motor skills and overall physical health. The intentional movement involved in dance therapy can help stabilize walking, improve balance, and enhance the quality of life for individuals facing such challenges.

In addition to these benefits, dance therapy has proven effective in trauma recovery. It provides a safe, structured, and supportive environment where trauma survivors can explore and express their feelings without having to articulate them verbally. Through dance, individuals can reclaim their bodily autonomy and begin to heal the disconnection between their bodies and minds often caused by traumatic experiences.

Overall, dance therapy represents a holistic approach to health and wellness, emphasizing the interconnectedness of physical movement and emotional health. Its accessibility and adaptability make it a versatile tool in the therapeutic realm, capable of addressing a wide range of mental health issues and promoting a deeper, more harmonious alignment between the body and mind. As it continues to gain recognition, dance therapy stands out as a poignant and powerful testament to the therapeutic potential of movement.

ᗞᗞᗞ

"Dance is the language of the soul, communicating through movements what cannot be said, stitching the fabric of our inner experiences into a tapestry of expressive motion."

♥♥♥

FOUR

Brushstrokes of the Mind: Painting as a Path to Healing

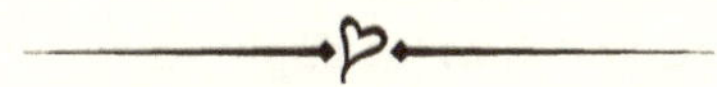

Painting, with its strokes, colors, and textures, offers a profound avenue for healing and emotional expression. As an art form, it transcends mere visual aesthetics, providing a therapeutic platform where individuals can explore and resolve deep emotional issues. This transformative process, often guided within the framework of art therapy, leverages the act of painting to facilitate personal growth, healing, and emotional well-being.

The therapeutic benefits of painting are grounded in its capacity to foster self-expression and creativity without the need for verbal communication. This aspect of painting is particularly vital for individuals who struggle with expressing their feelings and thoughts through words. By translating emotions into visual art, painters can externalize complex feelings, thus gaining new perspectives on their inner experiences. This process of creating visual manifestations of one's emotional state can be both enlightening and cathartic.

In therapeutic settings, painting is used as a tool to unlock emotional expression among those dealing with mental health disorders such as anxiety, depression, and post-traumatic stress disorder (PTSD). It provides a safe and controlled environment where individuals can explore painful memories or emotions at their own pace. The act of engaging with paints and canvas allows them to step back from their immediate emotional experiences and examine them from a new vantage point. This often leads to a greater understanding and processing of these emotions, contributing to recovery and healing.

Moreover, painting can significantly enhance cognitive functions. It involves a multitude of cognitive processes, including planning, problem-solving, and decision-making as the artist determines which colors to use and how to apply them to the canvas. This mental engagement can improve cognitive flexibility and foster a sharper mind. For elderly individuals, engaging in painting can be particularly beneficial as it helps maintain cognitive function and can even delay the progression of age-related cognitive disorders.

For individuals suffering from chronic illnesses or undergoing medical treatments, painting offers a form of psychological escape and relaxation. The focus required during the painting process can serve as a distraction from pain and discomfort, reducing the overall experience of suffering. Hospitals and healthcare settings often incorporate painting programs into patient care, recognizing its ability to improve mood and overall patient outlook.

Painting also plays a crucial role in enhancing self-esteem and confidence. The process of creating art allows individuals to achieve tangible results, which can be incredibly satisfying and bolster a sense of personal achievement. For many, seeing their progress and finished work gives them a boost in confidence, which can be particularly empowering for those who feel overwhelmed by their circumstances or conditions.

The social aspect of painting in group settings further amplifies its therapeutic value. Community painting classes or group therapy sessions provide individuals with opportunities to connect with others, share their experiences, and receive social support. These interactions can alleviate feelings of isolation and help build a supportive community that fosters emotional resilience.

For children and adolescents, painting can be an effective tool for emotional and social development. It helps them express emotions that they might not yet have the words to explain and can be a crucial outlet for processing their experiences. In educational settings, integrating painting into the curriculum can support emotional learning and improve students' attention and behavior.

The healing power of painting extends to those dealing with trauma. The non-verbal nature of painting allows trauma survivors to express their experiences without having to articulate them directly, which can be re-traumatizing. This makes painting an effective medium for gradually working through traumatic events in a controlled and safe manner.

In summary, painting stands out as a therapeutic medium that bridges the gap between emotional turmoil and expressive clarity. Its wide-ranging benefits touch on various aspects of mental and physical health, making it a versatile tool in therapeutic practices. As individuals continue to engage with painting, either personally or in therapeutic contexts, its role as a path to healing remains both significant and transformative. Its capacity to heal, soothe, and inspire is a testament to the profound impact that creative expression can have on the human spirit.

❧❧❧

"Every brushstroke carries a weight, a silent whisper of the artist's soul, transforming blank canvases into mirrors reflecting our own emotions."

♡♡♡

FIVE

THE SCULPTURE OF SERENITY: HOW 3D ART SHAPES OUR INNER PEACE

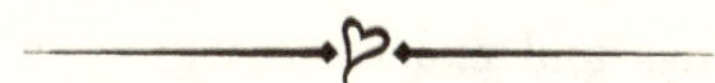

Sculpture, as a form of three-dimensional art, engages both the artist and the observer in a tangible interaction with form, space, and texture. This profound engagement with the physical world through sculpture can have a significant therapeutic impact, shaping the inner peace and emotional resilience of those involved. Sculptural art serves not just as a visual delight but as a medium for psychological and emotional healing, providing a physical space to process and express internal experiences.

The process of creating a sculpture involves a deeply immersive interaction with materials—be it clay, stone, metal, or wood—which requires mindfulness and presence. This focus pulls the sculptor into the moment, encouraging a state of flow where time and external worries recede, allowing for a peaceful engagement with the task at hand. For those creating or interacting with sculpture, this meditative process can reduce stress, enhance mindfulness, and promote a feeling of calm.

Sculpture's impact on inner peace can be attributed to its ability to manifest abstract emotions and thoughts into concrete forms. This externalization process is therapeutic as it provides a physical shape to internal feelings, making them more understandable and manageable. For individuals struggling with overwhelming emotions or traumatic memories, the ability to mold these into a physical form can be a powerful step towards healing. The act of sculpting allows them to 'release' these emotions into the artwork, facilitating a form of emotional catharsis.

In therapeutic settings, sculptural therapy is used to facilitate expression in a non-verbal way, which is particularly beneficial for those who find verbal expression challenging. It offers an alternative avenue for communication, where individuals can convey their feelings and experiences through the language of shapes and volumes. This form of expression can be particularly poignant for individuals dealing with mental health issues like depression, anxiety, or PTSD, providing a safe and controlled environment to explore complex feelings.

Moreover, engaging with sculpture can significantly enhance one's spatial reasoning and motor skills. The physical act of manipulating materials improves hand-eye coordination and fine motor skills, while conceptualizing three-dimensional forms boosts cognitive abilities related to spatial thinking. These skills are beneficial not only in artistic pursuits but also in everyday problem-solving and decision-making.

Sculpture also plays a crucial role in enhancing environmental mindfulness. By creating or placing sculptures in natural settings or spaces designed for reflection, such as gardens or meditation rooms, the art can alter one's perception of a space, inducing a sense of tranquility and mindfulness. These sculptures become focal points for meditation or contemplation, enriching the environment and providing a sanctuary for peaceful reflection.

The social component of sculptural art cannot be overlooked. Group sculptural projects or workshops can foster community and collaboration. In these social settings, participants share not only space and materials but also ideas and emotional support. This communal aspect of sculpture-making can be incredibly beneficial for building social connections and reducing feelings of isolation, which are often associated with mental health struggles.

For children and adolescents, sculpture offers a unique educational tool that combines learning with emotional development. Engaging young people in sculptural activities can help develop their creative thinking and problem-solving skills while also providing a healthy outlet for emotional expression. Through sculpture, children learn to appreciate art not just as observers but as creators, which can boost their self-esteem and confidence.

In therapeutic practices, especially those involving trauma survivors or individuals with significant emotional disturbances, sculpture therapy can act as a bridge to healing. By working with tangible materials, these individuals can regain a sense of control over their physical and emotional worlds. Sculpture allows them to reshape their narratives, quite literally, giving form to a new self-understanding and a reconstructed personal history that acknowledges their trauma without allowing it to dominate their lives.

In summary, the practice of sculpting not only shapes materials into art but also shapes the individuals who engage with it. Whether as creators or observers, participants in the world of sculpture find a unique pathway to serenity and personal growth. The physicality and tangibility of sculpture provide a unique medium through which one can explore complex emotions, enhance cognitive and motor skills, and foster personal and communal peace. This makes sculpture a potent tool in the quest for emotional well-being and inner peace, solidifying its role in art therapy and beyond.

ᏭᏭᏭ

"Music therapy isn't just about notes and melodies;
it's about unlocking the chambers of the heart that
have been sealed with pain, allowing healing to
flow through each beat."

❤❤❤

SIX

ECHOES OF THE SOUL: EXPLORING THE PSYCHOLOGICAL IMPACT OF SOUND

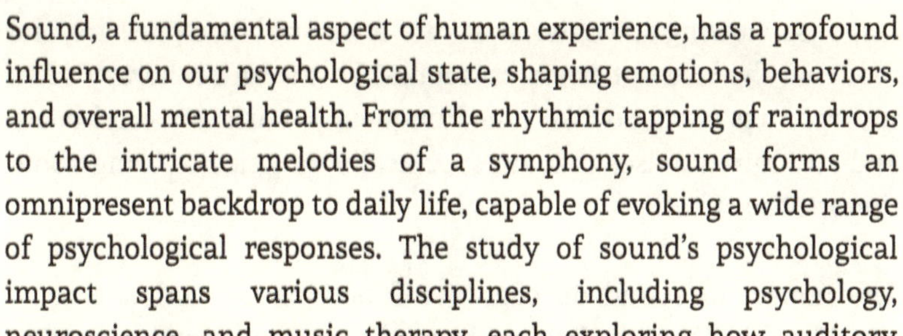

Sound, a fundamental aspect of human experience, has a profound influence on our psychological state, shaping emotions, behaviors, and overall mental health. From the rhythmic tapping of raindrops to the intricate melodies of a symphony, sound forms an omnipresent backdrop to daily life, capable of evoking a wide range of psychological responses. The study of sound's psychological impact spans various disciplines, including psychology, neuroscience, and music therapy, each exploring how auditory experiences influence human well-being.

At its core, the impact of sound on psychology is evident through its ability to alter mood states. Music, one of the most studied forms of sound, has the power to lift spirits, soothe nerves, and trigger complex emotional responses. It can energize, relax, or even move individuals to tears, demonstrating its potent effect on emotional regulation. The mechanism behind this involves the brain's limbic system, which is responsible for emotional processing. Sound waves influence this brain system, triggering the release of neurotransmitters like dopamine and serotonin, which are key players in mood regulation.

The therapeutic use of sound extends beyond music to include all auditory stimuli that promote healing and relaxation. This includes natural sounds, like the calming sound of waves or the soothing rustle of leaves, which have been shown to reduce stress, alleviate anxiety, and improve mental health. Nature soundscapes, for instance, are frequently used in meditation and relaxation practices to enhance the calming effects of these activities, grounding individuals in the present moment and facilitating a state of mental clarity and peace.

In clinical settings, sound therapy is employed to treat a range of psychological disorders. For those suffering from anxiety and stress-related disorders, sound therapy can offer significant relief. Certain frequencies and rhythms can influence the body's stress response, slowing down the heart rate, lowering blood pressure, and reducing the levels of stress hormones. This form of therapy often incorporates elements like tuned frequency music, binaural beats, and structured noises that are specifically designed to bring about therapeutic effects.

The impact of sound on cognitive functions is another area of considerable interest. Studies have shown that certain types of music can enhance cognitive performance, particularly in tasks involving memory and concentration. Classical music, often referred to as the "Mozart Effect," is reputed to enhance mental performance, though this effect is widely debated and thought to be more about mood improvement than direct cognitive enhancement.

However, the structured nature of certain musical pieces can facilitate more organized thinking and efficient information processing.

For individuals dealing with trauma or PTSD, sound therapy can be an invaluable tool. Traumatic events can disrupt the normal processing of sensory information. Through carefully controlled sound therapy, individuals can relearn how to process auditory inputs without the associated trauma responses. This is particularly effective in a technique known as sound desensitization, which gradually exposes individuals to sounds that might trigger traumatic memories in a controlled, safe environment, helping to reduce their traumatic reactions over time.

Sound's role in developmental and educational settings also highlights its psychological benefits. In young children, certain types of sound stimulation can aid developmental growth, influencing language acquisition and communication skills. Educational programs that integrate music and sound exploration can also enhance learning and retention, particularly in young children, by creating more engaging, dynamic, and memorable learning experiences.

Moreover, the communal aspects of sound, such as those experienced during concerts, festivals, or communal singing, play a significant role in social bonding and cultural identity. These events allow individuals to share emotional experiences through sound, fostering connections and strengthening community ties. The shared experience of sound can lead to collective catharsis and emotional synchronization, where groups of people experience emotions together, enhancing feelings of unity and belonging.

In therapeutic terms, the use of sound in group settings has shown benefits for enhancing interpersonal relationships and improving communication skills. Group therapy sessions that incorporate sound and music foster an environment of mutual respect and empathy, as participants express themselves and respond to others in a supportive setting. This can be particularly beneficial for those with social anxieties or difficulties in verbal communication.

In summary, the psychological impact of sound is vast and multifaceted, touching every aspect of human life from emotional expression and cognitive function to social interaction and cultural participation. The ability of sound to heal, soothe, and invigorate makes it a powerful tool in both everyday life and clinical practice. As research continues to uncover the depth of sound's influence on the human psyche, its application in therapy, education, and personal development is likely to expand, offering new ways to harness its benefits for mental health and well-being.

ϷϷϷ

"Through the act of creative writing, we map the
geography of our hearts, charting through words
the landscapes shaped by joy and scarred by
sorrow."

ᗡᗡᗡ

SEVEN

Stages of Recovery: Performance Arts as Therapeutic Practice

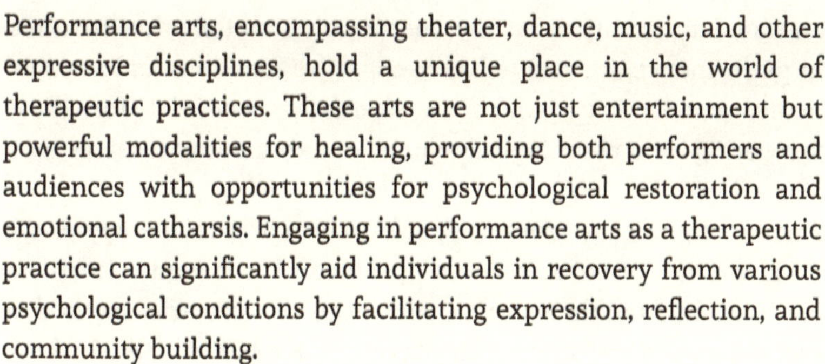

Performance arts, encompassing theater, dance, music, and other expressive disciplines, hold a unique place in the world of therapeutic practices. These arts are not just entertainment but powerful modalities for healing, providing both performers and audiences with opportunities for psychological restoration and emotional catharsis. Engaging in performance arts as a therapeutic practice can significantly aid individuals in recovery from various psychological conditions by facilitating expression, reflection, and community building.

The therapeutic benefits of performance arts stem largely from their ability to foster self-expression. For many dealing with emotional and psychological challenges, finding a voice to express complex feelings and experiences can be daunting. Performance arts create a structured yet flexible environment where individuals can explore and express emotions without the directness required in conventional talk therapy. This indirect approach can often make it easier for individuals to confront difficult emotions and disclose personal experiences.

In the context of therapy, the role-playing involved in performance arts allows individuals to step outside themselves and experiment with various perspectives and outcomes. This can be particularly transformative for those struggling with personal identity or those who feel stuck in rigid patterns of thinking and behavior. By adopting different roles, individuals can explore different facets of their personality and experience the emotional responses associated with these roles in a controlled, safe setting.

Moreover, performance arts often require a level of physical engagement that can be beneficial in itself. The physicality involved in dance and theater, for example, can improve physical health and enhance neurological function. This bodily engagement promotes the release of endorphins, the body's natural painkillers and mood elevators, which can provide relief from symptoms of depression and anxiety. Additionally, the coordination and rhythm required in performance arts can enhance cognitive functions and improve neural connectivity, which is especially beneficial for those recovering from neurological injuries or degenerative diseases.

Another significant aspect of performance arts in therapy is the development of narrative competence. Participants learn to construct and tell their stories, which can be a powerful method of reclaiming and reshaping their narratives. For individuals who have experienced trauma, the ability to narrate their experiences in a supportive environment can lead to greater insight and integration of their traumatic experiences. This storytelling process is not only cathartic but also helps individuals make sense of their past and envision a future beyond their current circumstances.

The communal nature of performance arts also plays a crucial role in therapeutic settings. These arts inherently involve collaboration and communication, fostering a sense of community and shared purpose among participants. This can be incredibly beneficial for individuals who often feel isolated due to their psychological issues. Being part of a group working towards a common goal can enhance social skills, improve communication abilities, and build trust among members. The supportive environment encourages a sense of belonging and collective accomplishment, which can be particularly empowering for those who may feel marginalized or disconnected from society.

Performance arts therapy also offers a unique avenue for emotion regulation. The process of preparing for a performance involves rehearsing expressions of emotion in a way that can help individuals gain control over their feelings. By repeatedly accessing and expressing various emotions in a safe environment, participants can learn to identify, understand, and manage their emotions more effectively. This rehearsal process can translate into better emotional regulation in daily life, as individuals become more accustomed to recognizing and coping with their feelings.

In educational and developmental contexts, performance arts have shown remarkable effectiveness in enhancing emotional and cognitive development among children and adolescents. These activities help young people develop empathy and emotional intelligence as they engage with diverse narratives and characters. For children with developmental disorders, performance arts can be particularly beneficial in improving social awareness and interaction skills.

Performance arts therapy is also utilized in the rehabilitation of offenders and in social rehabilitation programs, where it has been effective in reducing recidivism and aiding social reintegration. The structured yet expressive nature of these arts provides a constructive outlet for aggression and a platform for self-reflection and personal development.

Performance arts offer a rich, multifaceted therapeutic tool that can address a wide range of psychological and emotional issues. Whether it's through dance, drama, or music, the act of performing can transform lives by healing wounds, building bridges between individuals, and restoring emotional and psychological well-being. As more people engage with performance arts, either as participants or as part of an audience, its role as a profound therapeutic practice continues to grow, highlighting its importance in the healing arts.

♭♭♭

"The stage of performance is a sacred space where the echoes of personal transformation are felt, a place where characters are born from our vulnerabilities and strengths."

ᗰᗰᗰ

EIGHT

PHOTOGRAPHY AS REFLECTION: CAPTURING EMOTIONS THROUGH THE LENS

Photography, as an art form and a therapeutic tool, holds the power to capture and reflect the vast spectrum of human emotions. Through the lens, photographers not only freeze moments in time but also encapsulate feelings and stories, offering both the creator and the viewer a chance to explore and interpret underlying messages. The therapeutic benefits of photography are multifaceted, impacting psychological well-being by fostering mindfulness, self-expression, and a deeper connection with the world around us.

At its core, photography involves an act of focus not just of the camera lens, but of the mind. This process requires mindfulness, as the photographer must be fully present in the moment to capture the essence of their subject effectively. This necessity to live in the 'now' can be immensely beneficial for individuals dealing with anxiety or stress, as it encourages a mental state where worries about the past or future are pushed aside in favor of concentration on the current setting and subject. The mindful practice of photography can reduce symptoms of anxiety and depression, providing a calming influence and a temporary escape from life's pressures.

Furthermore, photography as a form of expression allows individuals to communicate feelings and experiences that might be hard to articulate with words. For those who experience emotional blockages or who cannot find the words to express their feelings, photography offers a visual language of communication. Capturing images that represent personal emotions or stories enables individuals to share their inner thoughts and feelings indirectly with others or even just with themselves, facilitating a form of emotional catharsis.

Photography also encourages individuals to see the world from different perspectives. By choosing what to include or exclude from the frame, photographers learn to look at their surroundings in new ways, noticing details that might otherwise be overlooked. This practice can lead to a greater appreciation of one's environment, fostering feelings of wonder and gratitude, which are linked to increased happiness and satisfaction with life.

The act of reviewing and editing photographs can further enhance self-reflection. As photographers examine their pictures, they have the opportunity to reflect on the moment captured, the emotions felt at the time, and the message they wish to convey through the image. This can be a powerful introspective tool that helps individuals understand their emotions and triggers, promoting greater self-awareness and emotional intelligence.

In therapeutic settings, photography can be used to help individuals process and document their personal journeys. In treatments for conditions like PTSD, for example, photography can assist individuals in reclaiming control of their narrative. By photographing personal environments or subjects that relate to their experiences, patients can externalize and examine their traumas in a safe and controlled manner, gradually reducing the emotional impact.

Photography's role in fostering community and social connections is also significant. Group photography projects or workshops can bring people together, providing a space for shared experiences and mutual understanding. For those feeling isolated, these communal activities can help form new relationships and strengthen existing ones, offering social support that is crucial for emotional health.

The accessibility of photography in the digital age means that more people than ever can explore its therapeutic benefits. With smartphones and digital cameras, individuals have the tools to engage with photography at almost any moment, providing a readily accessible means to enhance mental well-being. This democratization of photography allows a broad audience to explore the therapeutic potential of capturing images, making it a powerful tool for personal development and emotional healing.

Moreover, for individuals experiencing cognitive decline, such as the elderly or those with degenerative brain diseases, photography can serve as a cognitive exercise to help maintain cognitive functions. The process of taking and reviewing photos can stimulate memory recall and improve cognitive engagement.

In summary, photography offers a unique therapeutic avenue, blending art and mindfulness to enhance mental health and emotional well-being. Whether used as a professional therapeutic tool or a personal outlet, its capacity to capture and reflect emotions provides profound opportunities for growth and healing. As both an art form and a mode of expression, photography continues to offer insights into the human condition, fostering a deeper understanding of ourselves and the world we inhabit.

ᏬᏬᏬ

"In the quiet moments of painting, we find loud
revelations, the colors narrating stories of struggles
and triumphs that are universally understood."

♥♥♥

NINE

Art in Everyday Life: Integrating Creative Practices for Better Living

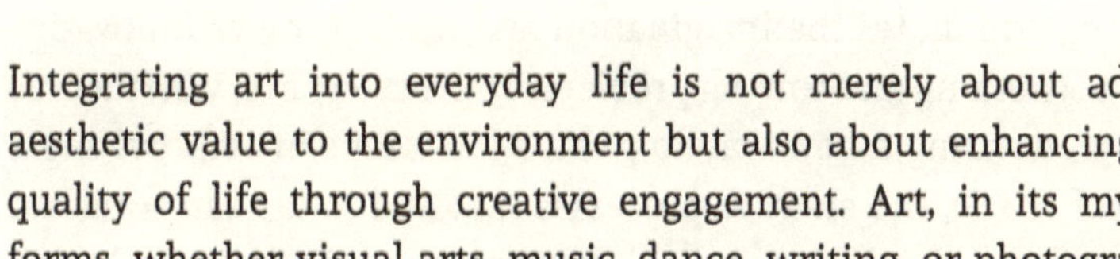

Integrating art into everyday life is not merely about adding aesthetic value to the environment but also about enhancing the quality of life through creative engagement. Art, in its myriad forms, whether visual arts, music, dance, writing, or photography, offers a unique source of enrichment and personal growth. By making art a regular part of daily routines, individuals can tap into a range of therapeutic benefits that promote mental health, foster creativity, and enhance emotional well-being.

At its most fundamental level, the inclusion of art in daily life encourages the expression of self and emotions in a manner that transcends verbal communication. Art provides a medium through which thoughts, feelings, and ideas can be explored and shared, offering a release and a way to process complex emotions. This form of expression can be particularly valuable for those who struggle with traditional forms of communication or for whom emotional expression feels daunting. Through art, individuals can find their voice and convey their inner thoughts in ways that words cannot capture.

Moreover, art enhances mindfulness and reduces stress. Activities like painting, drawing, or playing music require concentration and present-moment awareness, which are core aspects of mindfulness. These activities pull individuals away from their routine stressors and focus them on the task at hand, providing a break from the cycle of negative thoughts that often dominate minds under stress. The repetitive motions involved in creating art, such as the brushstrokes of a painter or the chords strummed by a guitarist, can serve as a meditative practice, soothing the mind and reducing overall stress levels.

Integrating art into daily life also boosts creativity and problem-solving skills. Engaging with art encourages divergent thinking—a way of exploring many solutions and possibilities. This kind of thinking stimulates the imagination and leads to more innovative ways of thinking and solving problems in everyday life. Whether it's through devising a new way to paint a landscape or improvising a piece of music, the creative processes involved in art can translate into enhanced ability to think creatively in personal and professional contexts.

Furthermore, art has the power to enhance one's aesthetic sensibility and appreciation for the surrounding world. Regular engagement with art makes one more observant and appreciative of minor details, whether in a well-designed building, an elegantly written piece of prose, or the intricate patterns found in nature. This heightened awareness can transform everyday experiences, making ordinary moments more enriching and fulfilling.

Socially, art can act as a bridge connecting individuals from different backgrounds and cultures. Shared artistic experiences, such as community theater productions, art exhibitions, or music concerts, provide opportunities for social interaction and community building. These events not only bring people together but also foster mutual understanding and respect among diverse groups, enhancing social cohesion and community spirit.

For families, incorporating art into home life can strengthen bonds and provide valuable learning experiences. Family art projects or music sessions can become cherished rituals that not only foster fun and creativity but also encourage teamwork and communication. For children, these activities are crucial for emotional and cognitive development, teaching skills such as cooperation, patience, and emotional expression.

In the workplace, art can be integrated to improve productivity and reduce stress. Offices adorned with art or those that incorporate music and other creative outputs can enhance the work environment, making it more stimulating and enjoyable for employees. Creative breaks, like drawing or doodling sessions, can rejuvenate the mind and lead to increased focus and productivity.

Integrating art into community spaces can also play a crucial role in enhancing the quality of life in neighborhoods. Public art installations, community murals, and local art fairs not only beautify spaces but also create focal points for community interaction and pride. These projects can revitalize areas, attract visitors, and promote a sense of pride and ownership among residents.

Integrating art into everyday life offers extensive benefits that extend well beyond simple enjoyment. From enhancing mental health and fostering creativity to enriching social interactions and community engagement, art plays a vital role in improving the quality of life. As more individuals and communities recognize and embrace the benefits of regular artistic engagement, art will continue to serve as a powerful tool for personal and communal development, transforming everyday experiences into opportunities for growth and connection.

❧❧❧

"When words are inadequate, let the arts speak;
dance, paint, and sing your emotions, for sometimes
the heart knows the rhythm better than the mind."

♡♡♡

TEN

RHYTHMS OF RECOVERY: DRUMMING AND PERCUSSION IN HEALING PROCESSES

Drumming and percussion instruments have been integral to human societies for millennia, serving not only as musical foundations but also as vital elements in ceremonial and healing traditions across cultures. Today, the therapeutic benefits of drumming are being increasingly recognized in modern medical and psychological circles, tapping into its primal power to heal, unite, and restore individuals dealing with various physical and emotional issues.

The act of drumming involves rhythmically striking a surface to produce sound, a simple action that yields complex benefits. One of the primary therapeutic aspects of drumming is its ability to reduce stress and anxiety. The physical activity of drumming releases endorphins, the body's natural feel-good chemicals, which can create feelings of euphoria and improve mood. This biochemical response is similar to the "runner's high" experienced during vigorous exercise, and it can be particularly potent in group drumming settings where the shared experience amplifies the emotional impact.

Moreover, drumming promotes relaxation through the induction of a meditative state. The repetitive nature of drumming can help shift the brain into a more relaxed state, reducing the levels of stress hormones like cortisol. This effect is enhanced by the focused attention required to maintain rhythm, which can act as a form of mindfulness practice, keeping individuals present and engaged in the moment, away from stressors and anxious thoughts.

Drumming has also been employed effectively in addressing emotional and behavioral issues. Participating in drum circles or therapeutic drumming sessions can provide an outlet for expression that might be inaccessible through traditional verbal therapy. It allows individuals to express feelings non-verbally, manage aggression, and explore complex emotions in a supportive, communal environment. This can be particularly beneficial for individuals with emotional dysregulation, such as those with PTSD or trauma-related disorders, as it provides a structured yet flexible outlet for emotional release.

In terms of physiological benefits, drumming can serve as a form of physical rehabilitation. The act requires coordination and motor skills, engaging not only the hands and arms but also the core and lower body, depending on the drumming style. For individuals recovering from physical injuries or neurological conditions, drumming can enhance motor control, coordination, and timing. This has been particularly noted in stroke rehabilitation, where rhythmic cues help improve gait and arm movement patterns.

Drumming also supports cognitive function and neurological health. The coordination required to maintain rhythm and tempo involves substantial cognitive engagement, activating various parts of the brain. Research has shown that engaging in musical activities such as drumming can enhance brain function, improve memory, and slow cognitive decline. For elderly individuals or those with conditions like Alzheimer's disease, drumming can provide cognitive stimulation that helps maintain brain health over time.

Social integration is another significant benefit of drumming. Group drumming can foster a sense of community and belonging, key components in emotional health and resilience. The synchronicity involved in playing rhythms together can enhance feelings of social connection and generate a shared experience that transcends cultural and personal barriers. This is particularly valuable for those who feel isolated or disconnected, as it provides an opportunity to engage with others in a meaningful and cooperative activity.

For children and adolescents, drumming can be a powerful tool for social and emotional development. It helps in building teamwork and social skills as young participants learn to listen to each other and synchronize their rhythms. Drumming can also boost confidence and self-esteem as children experience the joy of making music and contributing to a group performance.

Furthermore, drumming has unique cultural and spiritual dimensions that can enhance its therapeutic impact. In many cultures, drumming is seen as a pathway to spiritual growth and healing, connecting individuals to their cultural roots or spiritual practices. This cultural connection can add depth to the healing process, providing individuals with a sense of purpose and belonging that supports overall mental health.

In summary, drumming offers a versatile and accessible form of therapy that incorporates physical, cognitive, emotional, and social elements. Its rhythmic nature and the physical engagement it requires can help alleviate a host of psychological and physiological conditions, making it a powerful tool in therapeutic settings. As the understanding of its benefits continues to grow, drumming is likely to become an increasingly common feature in therapeutic practices, community settings, and individual health regimens, promoting healing and well-being through the universal language of rhythm.

"Art in therapy is the gentle guide, leading us through the mazes of our minds, shining a light on the darker corners where words fear to tread."

ԾԾԾ

ELEVEN

TALES OF TRANSFORMATION: STORYTELLING AND DRAMA THERAPY

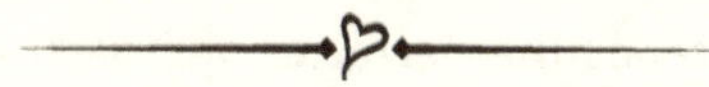

Storytelling and drama therapy are profound and dynamic tools used in therapeutic practices that tap into the ancient roots of narrative and performance to foster healing, personal growth, and psychological transformation. Both modalities use the structured yet flexible art of storytelling—whether spoken or acted out—to help individuals explore their lives, confront issues, and reshape their narratives. This therapeutic approach can be particularly effective in helping individuals process experiences, express emotions, and make profound life changes.

The Power of Narrative

At the heart of storytelling and drama therapy is the power of narrative. Humans are inherently storytelling creatures, constantly framing our experiences and identities through the stories we tell ourselves and others. In a therapeutic setting, storytelling allows individuals to externalize their inner experiences, giving them shape and form in a narrative structure. This process can be immensely cathartic, as it provides distance from the emotional intensity of personal experiences, allowing for easier handling and manipulation of those experiences.

Therapeutic storytelling can involve recounting personal stories, creating fictional tales, or reinterpreting old narratives that may have become harmful or limiting. By engaging with these narratives, individuals can gain new perspectives on their problems, viewing them through different lenses and exploring alternative outcomes. This can lead to significant shifts in self-perception and a reevaluation of personal beliefs and values.

Drama Therapy: Acting Out for Healing

Drama therapy extends the narrative approach into the realm of performance, using role-play, improvisation, and scripted performances to explore personal issues and relationships. This form of therapy provides a unique opportunity for individuals to literally 'act out' their internal conflicts and aspirations. By stepping into different roles, patients can experience a range of perspectives and emotions safely and constructively. This can be particularly powerful for exploring complex interpersonal dynamics or confronting parts of the self that are usually repressed or ignored.

In drama therapy, the stage becomes a safe space where anything can happen. This freedom allows individuals to experiment with emotional responses and behavioral strategies in a controlled environment. Such role-play can be revelatory, providing insights that are transferable to real-life situations. Moreover, drama therapy can help build confidence and social skills, as individuals learn to express themselves more freely and react to others in the moment.

Therapeutic Performance

One of the most potent aspects of drama therapy is the therapeutic performance, where therapy participants prepare and present a piece of drama to an audience. This process combines the cathartic benefits of both storytelling and performance, as individuals craft a narrative that holds personal significance and then embody that narrative through their performance. The act of performing one's story in front of others can be a powerful affirmation of one's experiences and emotions, providing a sense of validation and shared understanding that is often crucial for emotional healing.

Re-authoring Self-Narratives

Both storytelling and drama therapy are centered on the concept of 're-authoring' one's narrative. Many individuals come into therapy with narratives that cast them in passive or victimized roles—stories that may have been internalized based on past traumas or societal messages. Through storytelling and drama, these individuals can begin to see themselves as active agents in their stories, capable of overcoming obstacles and effecting change in their lives. This shift from a passive to an active role in one's narrative is often a critical step in recovery and personal development.

Community and Collective Healing

Storytelling and drama therapy also have a strong communal aspect, as they often involve groups of people sharing stories and performing together. This collective dimension can foster a strong sense of community and support among participants, as they work together to create and share their stories. The group setting provides a network of empathy and understanding, where individual experiences are honored and shared, reducing feelings of isolation and promoting a sense of belonging.

Applications Across Populations

The versatility of storytelling and drama therapy makes them suitable for a wide range of populations, including children, adolescents, adults, and the elderly. These therapies can be particularly impactful for children and teenagers, who often use play naturally to understand the world and can benefit greatly from the playful yet profound nature of drama therapy. In geriatric populations, storytelling can help preserve personal identity and continuity of self, especially in individuals facing memory loss or cognitive decline.

In conclusion, storytelling and drama therapy offer powerful pathways for emotional and psychological healing. Through the creation and enactment of personal and collective narratives, individuals can explore their identities, confront their issues, and transform their lives. These therapies harness the innate human capacity for narrative and performance, making them accessible and effective tools for therapists aiming to facilitate deep and lasting change in their clients.

ᐠᐠᐠ

"Photography captures not just images but
emotions, freezing moments of feeling that beg to be
remembered, immortalizing whispers of the soul."

❥❥❥

TWELVE

THE ARCHITECTURE OF HARMONY: BUILDING SPACES FOR MENTAL HEALTH

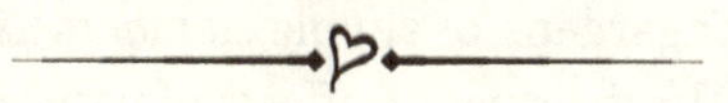

The concept of architectural psychology, which explores the impact of built environments on human behavior and mental well-being, has gained significant traction in recent years. Understanding how physical spaces influence emotions, thoughts, and behaviors can play a crucial role in designing environments that promote mental health and well-being. This field intertwines architecture, interior design, environmental psychology, and neuroscience to create spaces—whether homes, workplaces, schools, or therapeutic facilities—that are not only functional and aesthetically pleasing but also conducive to mental and emotional health.

Principles of Design for Mental Well-being

The design of a space can profoundly affect the mental states of its users. Certain key principles, when thoughtfully applied, can enhance the psychological comfort and therapeutic qualities of environments. Natural light, for instance, is a critical component. Numerous studies have shown that exposure to natural light can boost mood, improve sleep, and increase productivity. By incorporating large windows, skylights, and strategically placed mirrors to enhance natural light, architects can create spaces that naturally elevate mood and energy levels.

Another important principle is the use of nature and natural elements within architectural design, often referred to as biophilic design. This approach is based on the inherent human tendency to connect with nature. Introducing plant life, water features, and views of natural settings can reduce stress, enhance creativity, and improve cognitive function. Even in urban settings, integrating green roofs, indoor gardens, or simple elements like wood and stone can help recreate the therapeutic effects of nature.

Spatial configuration also plays a significant role in shaping mental health. Open spaces that promote social interaction can help alleviate feelings of isolation and depression. However, it is equally important to include private, quiet areas where individuals can retreat for solitude and reflection. The balance between community and privacy in architectural design can support varied mental health needs, catering to both extroverted and introverted behaviors.

Color Psychology in Architecture

The colors used in a space can have a dramatic impact on a person's psychological state. Color psychology in architecture considers how different hues can affect feelings and behaviors. For example, blues and greens are often associated with calmness and can be used in areas designed for relaxation or stress relief. Warm colors like yellows and oranges can stimulate conversation and are beneficial in communal areas to promote social interactions.

Acoustic Design for Mental Health

Sound environment is another critical factor in architectural design for mental health. Poor acoustic design can lead to a noisy environment, which increases stress and decreases concentration. Incorporating soundproofing materials, designing spaces that minimize echo, and including elements that absorb sound can create quieter, more peaceful environments conducive to mental well-being.

Inclusive and Accessible Design

Inclusive design ensures that spaces are accessible to everyone, regardless of age, disability, or other factors. This approach not only meets legal requirements but also promotes mental health by ensuring that all individuals feel welcomed and capable of using the space without undue stress or hardship. Features such as ramps, non-slip surfaces, and ample lighting can make environments safer and more comfortable for everyone, particularly for those with physical limitations or the elderly.

Therapeutic Spaces in Healthcare Design

In healthcare facilities, where the need for therapeutic environments is most critical, the design can significantly influence patient recovery and staff well-being. Patient rooms with views of nature, art installations, and interiors with homelike designs can contribute to faster recovery rates and reduce the need for pain medication. For mental health facilities, creating non-institutional environments with opportunities for both social interaction and private reflection can aid in the treatment process and reduce the stigma associated with mental health care.

Designing for Educational and Workplace Well-being

Schools and workplaces also benefit from architectural designs that consider mental health. Educational spaces that are bright, airy, and connected to outdoor areas can enhance learning and concentration, while reducing stress and anxiety among students. Workplaces designed with flexible work areas that allow for customization, relaxation zones, and opportunities for informal interaction can reduce burnout and promote productivity.

The architecture of harmony involves creating spaces that go beyond aesthetic and functional considerations to address the psychological and emotional needs of their users. By incorporating principles of natural light, biophilic design, color psychology, acoustic planning, inclusive access, and thoughtful spatial configuration, architects and designers can craft environments that significantly improve mental health outcomes. As awareness of the psychological impact of architectural design grows, the creation of harmonious spaces that support mental well-being is becoming a critical aspect of modern architecture and design.

ᗪᗪᗪ

"A simple melody can be a bridge between minds, a
universal language that heals divides, stitching
together disparate hearts with threads of harmony."

❥❥❥

THIRTEEN

Cinema and Psyche: Film as a Tool for Emotional Exploration

Cinema, with its powerful blend of visuals, dialogue, music, and narrative, holds a unique position as a medium of profound emotional and psychological impact. Films do more than entertain; they offer rich insights into human conditions and provide a mirror to the viewer's own emotions and experiences. The role of film as a tool for emotional exploration is significant in both therapeutic contexts and everyday life, enhancing our understanding of ourselves and others.

The Psychological Impact of Film

Film's ability to evoke emotions is one of its most compelling characteristics. A well-crafted movie can make audiences laugh, cry, feel fear, or experience relief, often within the span of two hours. This emotional journey is not just a passive experience but an active engagement that can lead to profound cathartic effects. By identifying with characters, experiencing narrative developments, and reacting to the cinematic techniques used to tell the story, viewers can undergo emotional catharsis, releasing suppressed emotions in a safe and contained environment.

Empathy and Identification

One of the key aspects of cinema as a therapeutic tool is its ability to foster empathy. Films allow viewers to step into the shoes of characters from different backgrounds, cultures, and life situations, offering perspectives that they might never encounter in their daily lives. This can broaden understanding and tolerance, reduce prejudices, and promote a sense of shared humanity. Through the process of identification with characters, viewers can also experience emotional growth. Seeing a character navigate a challenging situation can inspire, offer solace, and sometimes provide solutions to real-life problems.

Narrative Therapy

Films are often used in narrative therapy, where stories are utilized to help clients gain insight into their lives. Movies can serve as metaphors for clients' experiences, helping them to reframe their own narratives in more empowering ways. Therapists might use specific films to help clients discuss difficult subjects, or to inspire them to change their own life narratives. For example, a character's journey through grief and ultimate acceptance might help someone struggling with loss to find a path forward.

Mirror to Society

Cinema also acts as a cultural mirror, reflecting societal issues, norms, and conflicts. Films that tackle social issues—such as inequality, racism, or mental illness—can initiate important conversations and encourage viewers to reflect on their own views and behaviors. This reflective process is essential for both personal and societal growth, as it challenges entrenched beliefs and fosters a more nuanced understanding of complex issues.

Psychological Resilience and Growth

Films can also contribute to psychological resilience by providing models of coping and survival. Characters that overcome adversity can serve as sources of inspiration. For individuals facing similar challenges, these stories can be motivational, showing that resilience and persistence can lead to overcoming obstacles. Additionally, seeing various adaptive coping mechanisms in films can provide viewers with strategies that they might apply in their own lives.

Educational Tool

Beyond therapy, cinema is an educational tool that can teach about different psychological states, disorders, and therapies. Educational films designed to explain psychological concepts or to depict the lived experience of mental health issues can enhance viewers' understanding of these conditions, reducing stigma and supporting better mental health practices.

Community and Connection

Watching films can also be a communal activity that strengthens bonds between people. Film screenings in community centers, schools, or even outdoor parks bring people together, sharing a collective experience that can foster a sense of community and belonging. Discussions that arise from these shared viewing experiences can enhance social ties and contribute to a supportive community environment.

Film Festivals and Advocacy

Film festivals often highlight films that address specific themes, including those related to mental health and emotional wellness. These festivals can act as advocacy platforms, raising awareness about the issues depicted and promoting societal change. They can also provide filmmakers and audiences with opportunities to engage directly with these issues through panels, discussions, and workshops.

Cinema offers a unique and powerful tool for emotional exploration, psychological education, and social commentary. Its ability to combine narrative, music, and visual storytelling into a cohesive whole makes it an effective medium for exploring complex emotional and psychological landscapes. Whether used within therapeutic settings to facilitate emotional healing and growth or enjoyed as part of community activities, films continue to offer valuable insights into the human psyche, promoting both personal introspection and broader societal understanding.

"Sculpture is both an act of creation and discovery; in every block of marble resides a story, and with each chip, we uncover more of our shared humanity."

ᗜᗜᗜ

FOURTEEN

FABRIC OF FEELINGS: TEXTILE ARTS AND THEIR THERAPEUTIC EFFECTS

Textile arts, encompassing a wide range of activities such as weaving, knitting, embroidery, and quilting, have been a part of human culture for millennia, serving both utilitarian and expressive purposes. In recent years, the therapeutic potentials of these crafts have been increasingly recognized, contributing not only to the aesthetic and cultural realms but also to mental health and wellbeing. The act of working with textiles provides numerous psychological benefits, including stress reduction, improved mood, enhanced cognitive function, and a strengthened sense of community.

The Meditative Quality of Textile Arts

One of the primary therapeutic aspects of textile arts is their inherent meditative quality. The repetitive motions involved in knitting, sewing, or weaving are rhythmically soothing and can induce a meditative state that lowers stress and anxiety levels. This repetitive action helps focus the mind on the present moment, distracting it from distressing thoughts and allowing for a form of mindfulness practice. For many people, these activities provide a peaceful retreat from the chaos of everyday life, offering a chance to slow down and engage in a calming, focused task.

Cognitive Benefits and Mental Agility

Engaging in textile arts also offers significant cognitive benefits. These crafts require concentration, pattern recognition, and problem-solving skills, all of which serve to keep the mind engaged and active. Following complex patterns in knitting or embroidery, for example, can enhance mental agility and attention to detail. For older adults, engaging in these activities can be particularly beneficial, helping to maintain mental acuity and possibly delay the cognitive decline associated with aging.

Emotional Expression Through Textiles

Textile arts provide a powerful medium for emotional expression. The choice of colors, patterns, and textures can be deeply symbolic, offering a non-verbal mode of expression that can be especially valuable for those who find it difficult to articulate feelings through words. For individuals dealing with emotional trauma or mental health issues, creating something tangible like a quilt or a garment can be an empowering way to reclaim control over their environment and emotions. The finished product stands as a visual representation of personal feelings and experiences, which can be particularly validating and cathartic.

Healing Through the Sense of Touch

The tactile nature of textile arts plays a significant role in their therapeutic value. Touch is a fundamental human need, and engaging with various fabrics can provide comfort and sensory stimulation that is soothing and reassuring. For individuals with sensory processing disorders, the varied textures of textile materials can be used therapeutically to stimulate or calm the sensory system as needed.

Building Community and Social Bonds

Textile arts often involve a community component, whether through classes, workshops, or informal crafting groups. These social settings provide opportunities for sharing skills, offering encouragement, and fostering connections with others who have similar interests. For many, these communities become a vital source of social support and friendship, which are essential for mental health and well-being. The act of creating together can strengthen bonds and provide a sense of belonging and achievement.

Therapeutic Programs and Initiatives

Numerous programs and initiatives have recognized the therapeutic benefits of textile arts, integrating them into mental health therapies, community centers, and schools. In mental health settings, patients may be encouraged to engage in textile arts as a way to manage symptoms of depression, anxiety, or PTSD. Educational programs might incorporate these crafts into curricula to enhance fine motor skills, concentration, and emotional regulation among students.

Sustainability and Mindfulness

In an era increasingly aware of environmental impact, textile arts can also contribute to sustainable practices. Many enthusiasts take up recycling and upcycling projects, transforming old clothes or textiles into new creations. This aspect of textile arts not only reduces waste but can also instill a sense of purpose and responsibility, adding another layer of meaning to the craft.

The therapeutic effects of textile arts are multifaceted, blending psychological, cognitive, and social benefits. These crafts offer a unique combination of meditative repetition, tactile engagement, creative expression, and communal activity, making them a potent tool for improving mental health and enhancing quality of life. As these benefits become more widely recognized, textile arts are likely to play an increasingly prominent role in therapeutic settings, community programs, and personal wellness routines, helping individuals weave a fabric of feelings into a tapestry of healing and resilience.

 PPP

"Let dance be your diary, each movement a word, each routine a page, telling the story of who you are in the language of rhythm and grace."

💗💗💗

FIFTEEN

MELODIES OF THE MIND: THE PSYCHOLOGY BEHIND MUSIC THERAPY

Music therapy is an established clinical intervention that uses music to address physical, emotional, cognitive, and social needs of individuals. Through both active and receptive techniques, it can support numerous mental health conditions, enhance brain functions, and significantly improve quality of life. This therapeutic approach integrates neuroscience, psychology, and musicology, offering a profound understanding of how music can be harnessed for therapeutic benefits.

Foundations of Music Therapy

Music therapy is based on the understanding that all individuals respond to music on some level, even if they are not musically inclined or lack musical training. At its core, the practice involves creating, singing, moving to, and listening to music. It is facilitated by a credentialed therapist who tailors the sessions to the individual's specific needs and health objectives. This personalization makes music therapy applicable to a wide range of scenarios and conditions, including developmental and learning disabilities, neurological conditions, chronic illnesses, and mental disorders such as depression and anxiety.

Emotional Regulation and Expression

One of the most significant applications of music therapy lies in the domain of emotional health. Music has a unique ability to modulate moods and emotions, tapping into deep emotional responses without need for direct verbal communication. It can evoke memories, enhance mood, soothe agitation, and provide an outlet for expression. For individuals experiencing emotional and behavioral difficulties, music therapy offers a way to express feelings safely and constructively, often allowing emotions to surface and be understood and processed more effectively than through words alone.

Neurological Impact of Music

Music has a profound effect on the brain, influencing areas involved in mood regulation, stress levels, and cognitive function. Neurological music therapy is particularly focused on how music impacts brain processes through neuroplasticity—the brain's ability to reorganize itself by forming new neural connections. This aspect is crucial for patients recovering from brain injuries or those who suffer from neurodegenerative diseases. Music therapy has been shown to improve outcomes in stroke recovery, Parkinson's disease, and Alzheimer's disease, facilitating movement, improving cognitive function, and reducing symptoms of depression and anxiety.

Music and Stress Reduction

Listening to music can significantly decrease the levels of the stress hormone cortisol in the body, which is why music therapy is often utilized to manage stress. Therapeutic music sessions typically involve techniques such as guided meditation with background music or active engagement in making music to distract and calm the mind. For individuals struggling with chronic stress, anxiety disorders, or conditions like PTSD, music therapy can provide a profound sense of relief and tranquility.

Cognitive Enhancement Through Music

Music therapy also offers cognitive benefits, particularly in terms of enhanced memory and improved attention span. For children and adults with attention deficit disorders or learning disabilities, music therapy can improve concentration and lengthen periods of focus. Music's structure helps to organize the cognitive system, providing a rhythm that guides neural activity. For the elderly, engaging in music therapy can be a protective factor against the decline in memory and cognitive function associated with aging.

Social Integration and Communication

For individuals with autism spectrum disorder or social communication difficulties, music therapy can enhance communication skills. It provides a structured environment where social cues are paired with musical activities, facilitating understanding and interaction in a non-verbal manner. Group music therapy sessions also promote social interaction and cohesion, helping participants improve their ability to work in groups, understand social norms, and express themselves within a social context.

Personal Development and Self-Esteem

Participating in music therapy can significantly boost self-esteem and confidence. Learning to play an instrument, compose a song, or perform in a group setting provides accomplishments that foster pride and self-confidence. For individuals facing emotional challenges, the mastery of musical skills can provide a meaningful achievement and a sense of identity.

Cultural and Spiritual Dimensions

Music is deeply rooted in cultural and spiritual traditions, which enhances the therapeutic impact of music therapy by connecting individuals to their cultural background or spiritual beliefs. This connection can be particularly comforting and grounding for individuals dealing with existential issues or cultural displacement.

Music therapy offers a versatile and effective approach to health and well-being. Through the careful clinical use of musical interventions, music therapists help individuals manage a host of issues across emotional, cognitive, physical, and social domains. As understanding and appreciation of the psychological impact of music continue to grow, music therapy is increasingly recognized as a profound and essential component of modern therapeutic practices.

♭♭♭

"Film is a powerful medium that mirrors life,
transforming the silver screen into a canvas where
our deepest fears and highest hopes are projected."

♥♥♥

SIXTEEN

COLORS OF CALM: CHOOSING PALETTES FOR PSYCHOLOGICAL WELL-BEING

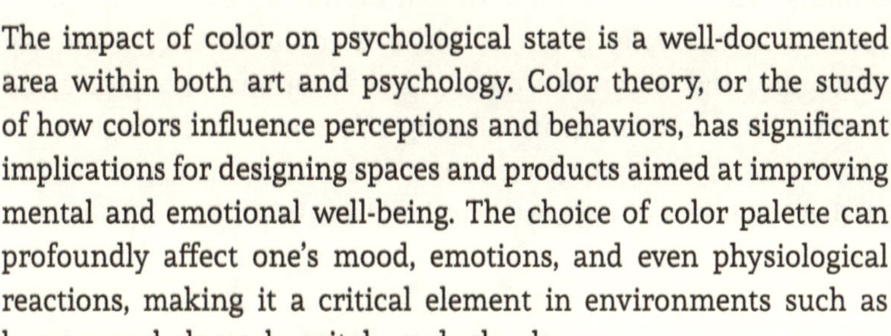

The impact of color on psychological state is a well-documented area within both art and psychology. Color theory, or the study of how colors influence perceptions and behaviors, has significant implications for designing spaces and products aimed at improving mental and emotional well-being. The choice of color palette can profoundly affect one's mood, emotions, and even physiological reactions, making it a critical element in environments such as homes, workplaces, hospitals, and schools.

Understanding Color Psychology

Color psychology is the science of how colors affect human behavior and mood. Each color has different wavelengths and energies, which are believed to trigger certain responses in the brain. These responses can influence psychological states and evoke specific emotions. For instance, blue is often associated with calmness and serenity, while red can trigger feelings of passion or aggression. Understanding these effects allows designers, architects, and even individuals to use colors to their advantage in creating spaces that enhance well-being.

The Impact of Color on Mood and Emotion

The use of color to influence mood is well-established. Warm colors, such as red, orange, and yellow, can evoke feelings of warmth and comfort but also anger and hostility if too dominant. Cool colors like blue, green, and purple generally promote calm and are thought to be soothing. For environments where stress reduction is critical, such as hospitals or mental health clinics, these colors are frequently utilized to create a tranquil atmosphere.

Therapeutic Use of Colors

In therapeutic settings, colors are strategically employed to have calming effects, reduce anxiety, and even alter the perception of space. For example, green is often used in settings requiring tranquility and restoration due to its associations with nature and growth. Blue, known for its calming effect, is ideal for high-stress environments like emergency rooms or examination areas. The use of these colors can support emotional healing and contribute to overall stress reduction.

Colors in Learning and Educational Spaces

Educational psychology has explored the role of colors in learning environments, finding that certain colors can enhance concentration and learning efficiency. For example, color palettes that include soft blues and greens are often used in classrooms to create a calm and focused atmosphere conducive to learning. Brighter colors, like yellow, can be energizing and are sometimes used in areas where creativity or physical activity is encouraged.

Color in Workspaces

The design of workspaces often incorporates color psychology to boost productivity and employee satisfaction. Colors like blue and green can enhance focus and efficiency, making them suitable for task-oriented work environments. On the other hand, areas designed for brainstorming or collaborative work might feature brighter, more stimulating colors such as orange or light red, which can foster creativity and energy.

Influence of Color on Physical Health

The influence of color extends beyond psychological well-being to physical health. For instance, exposure to certain colors can influence physiological processes such as blood pressure and metabolism. Red, often associated with increased heart rate, might be used sparingly in places where calm is essential. Conversely, blue lighting has been used in certain environments to calm patients and even reduce pain perception.

Personal Spaces and Color Choices

When it comes to personal spaces like homes, color choice becomes a highly personal decision that reflects individual preferences and emotional needs. People often choose colors for their living spaces based on how they want to feel in those environments. For example, bedrooms might be painted in cool, pastel shades to promote relaxation and sleep, while living areas might feature warmer tones to foster sociability and warmth.

Cultural Considerations in Color Psychology

It's important to note that color perceptions can vary significantly across cultures, which affects how colors are used in space design globally. For example, while white is often associated with purity and cleanliness in many Western cultures, it may be associated with mourning and death in some Eastern cultures. This cultural dimension must be considered when designing public spaces or products intended for international markets.

Future Trends in Color Psychology

As more is understood about the relationship between color and psychological function, future trends in interior design, architecture, and art will likely continue to integrate color psychology principles more deeply into their practices. Innovations in lighting and digital displays that can change color dynamically offer new ways to utilize color therapy in everyday environments, potentially leading to environments that adapt to the emotional needs of their users.

In conclusion, the strategic use of colors can play a pivotal role in enhancing psychological well-being and emotional health. From the calming hues used in a therapist's office to the vibrant colors energizing a fitness center, understanding and applying color psychology can transform ordinary spaces into environments that support and nurture psychological and physical health.

ᗧᗧᗧ

"Drawing is not just about lines and shapes; it's about setting emotions free, giving them form and color, and learning the contours of our own feelings."

ᕥᕥᕥ

SEVENTEEN

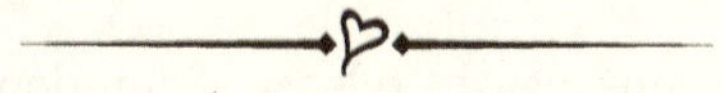

Creative writing has long been recognized as a powerful form of self-expression and emotional exploration. It serves as a cathartic outlet for personal feelings and experiences, offering writers a means to articulate what might otherwise remain unspoken or unprocessed. Through poetry, narrative fiction, personal essays, and other forms of written art, individuals can explore and convey complex emotions, often leading to significant psychological relief and insight.

The Therapeutic Power of Writing

The process of writing can be inherently therapeutic. It provides a safe space where individuals can confront painful memories, articulate deep-seated fears, and celebrate personal triumphs. The act of putting thoughts and emotions into words challenges writers to think deeply about their experiences, leading to increased self-awareness and often a new understanding of a past event. This act of shaping and reshaping thoughts through language allows individuals to gain control over their emotions and begin the process of healing.

For many, the therapeutic benefits of writing include the management of their emotional health through regular reflection and expression. Writing about traumatic experiences, in particular, can reduce the power of those memories by transforming the narrative into something tangible that can be analyzed and understood. Studies have shown that writing about one's feelings can significantly improve mental health by reducing stress, anxiety, and depression.

Writing as a Form of Emotional Release

Creative writing encourages the release of emotion, not just through the act of writing itself but through the creative process that underpins the crafting of narratives and poems. This process involves tapping into different layers of emotion and memory, weaving these elements into a coherent piece that speaks to both the author and the reader. For individuals dealing with grief, loss, or trauma, creative writing provides a conduit for expressing pain and complex emotions, offering a way to work through and eventually move past these feelings.

The physical act of writing—whether by hand or typing—also plays a role in catharsis. It engages the brain in a focused activity, demanding attention to detail and immersion in the task, which can distract from immediate emotional distress and provide a break from rumination.

Exploring the Self Through Creative Writing

Creative writing often involves exploration of the self. Writers may create characters who reflect their traits or experiences, or they may write from perspectives that allow them to step outside their own lives. Through characters and fictional scenarios, writers can confront emotional realities in a controlled and bounded environment, experimenting with different outcomes or responses to scenarios that parallel their own lives.

This vicarious exploration can lead to deeper empathy for oneself and others, as well as a greater understanding of human motives and vulnerabilities. For those undergoing therapy, creative writing can supplement more traditional treatments by providing another layer of insight into personal behaviors and thought patterns.

Community and Connection in Writing

Beyond the personal benefits, creative writing often draws people together into supportive communities. Workshops, writing groups, and online forums offer spaces where writers can share their work and receive feedback in a supportive environment. These communities can be particularly valuable for individuals who feel isolated due to mental health issues or life circumstances. The sense of belonging and understanding that comes from sharing one's writing can reinforce feelings of self-worth and resilience.

Writing to Reclaim Power

Creative writing empowers writers to reclaim control over their narratives. For individuals who have experienced trauma or loss, the ability to shape the story of those experiences can be a powerful act of reclamation. Writing provides the tools to redefine personal histories, transforming a narrative of victimhood into one of survival and strength.

Educational and Developmental Benefits

Creative writing also has significant educational and developmental benefits. It enhances cognitive and communication skills, including vocabulary, grammar, and organizational abilities. For children and adolescents, creative writing can be a way of developing these skills while also exploring personal identity and emotional maturity.

Promoting Mental Health and Well-Being

In therapeutic settings, clinicians may use writing tasks as part of treatment for mental health disorders. Assignments might include writing letters that will never be sent, keeping a daily journal, or crafting stories that involve coping mechanisms for characters that mirror the writer's own challenges. These exercises can help individuals process emotions and develop healthier coping strategies.

Creative writing as a form of catharsis represents a profound and versatile tool for emotional healing. It offers individuals a means to express and reshape their experiences and emotions, contributing not only to personal insight and growth but also to a greater sense of control and empowerment over their lives. As more people turn to writing to pen down their pain, the link between creative expression and mental health continues to strengthen, highlighting the essential role of the arts in fostering well-being and resilience.

ᐯᐯᐯ

"Theater is the alchemy of the human experience, turning the raw materials of our emotions into golden moments of insight and connection."

❧❧❧

EIGHTEEN

THE PLAY OF LIGHT: HOW LIGHTING IN ART INFLUENCES MOOD AND MIND

Lighting, whether in art, architecture, or everyday settings, profoundly impacts human psychology, influencing mood, perception, and even well-being. The way light interacts with spaces and objects can transform our experience of them, evoking different emotions and altering our perceptions. In the realm of art, lighting is not just a technical requirement; it is an artistic tool that shapes how we experience and interpret artworks. Understanding the psychological effects of light is crucial for artists, designers, and architects who manipulate light to create specific atmospheres and emotional responses.

Psychological Impact of Light

Light affects us on a biological and psychological level. Natural light, for instance, is known to boost mood and productivity and plays a crucial role in regulating our circadian rhythms. In artificial settings, the intensity, color temperature, and direction of light can also influence these aspects significantly. Bright, cool lights are typically energizing and can enhance concentration and alertness. In contrast, warm, dim lights are soothing and relaxing, often used in environments where calmness is desired.

Lighting in Visual Art

In visual arts, lighting serves as a powerful narrative device. Artists use light and shadow to direct viewers' attention, highlight emotional elements of a scene, and convey specific moods. The use of chiaroscuro, a technique that employs stark light contrasts to create a dramatic effect, is an example of how lighting can enhance the emotional impact of art. This technique not only emphasizes the physical form through high contrast but also enriches the narrative depth, often evoking a sense of mystery or solemnity.

Light as a Symbol in Art

Light often carries symbolic meanings in various cultural contexts. It can represent purity, hope, revelation, and intellect, among other concepts. Artists might manipulate light to symbolize these themes or to create a dialogue with the viewer that transcends the literal components of the artwork. In religious art, for instance, light frequently symbolizes divine presence or spiritual enlightenment, guiding the viewer's interpretation toward a deeper, spiritual narrative.

Emotional Responses to Light

The emotional responses elicited by different lighting setups are not merely subjective but are often shared across human cultures. For example, low lighting can create an atmosphere of intimacy and privacy, while bright lighting can make a space feel more open and safe. These reactions are partly evolutionary, as human vision and emotional responses have developed to react to lighting cues—bright light typically indicates daylight and safety, whereas darkness can signify danger.

Therapeutic Effects of Light in Art Installations

Art installations that manipulate light can have therapeutic effects. These installations often create immersive environments that can alter one's mood or emotional state. For instance, James Turrell's light installations play with space and perception, often evoking profound tranquility and awe. The controlled lighting environments in such installations can lead viewers to experience a range of emotions, from calmness and introspection to joy and wonder.

Lighting in Performance Art

In performance art, lighting is crucial in setting the tone and guiding the audience's emotional journey. It can isolate performers, enhance the drama, or soften a scene. Changes in lighting can signal shifts in narrative or emotional intensity, helping to tell the story without words. In dance and theater, lighting designers collaborate closely with directors and choreographers to ensure that light supports the artistic intentions, enhancing both the performances and the audience's emotional experience.

Architectural Lighting

In architecture, the strategic use of lighting can transform physical spaces to influence mood and behavior. Architects consider natural and artificial lighting at the design stage, aiming to create spaces that feel inviting, functional, and aesthetically pleasing. Well-lit spaces are often perceived as safer and more welcoming, whereas poorly lit areas can evoke feelings of anxiety and discomfort. The inclusion of skylights, large windows, and thoughtful artificial lighting are all techniques used to harness the psychological benefits of light.

Interactive and Dynamic Lighting

With advancements in technology, interactive and dynamic lighting systems have become more prevalent in art and architectural design. These systems can respond to human activity or environmental changes, altering lighting based on the presence or behavior of people, which can enhance user experience and engagement. Such adaptive lighting not only conserves energy but also tailors the emotional and aesthetic experience of a space to its occupants, enhancing comfort and satisfaction.

The manipulation of light within art and architectural spaces holds significant sway over our psychological and emotional states. From setting the mood in a gallery to enhancing the functionality of a workspace, the strategic use of light is integral to creating environments that positively influence the human experience. As we continue to understand the intricate ways in which light affects us, the potential to harness this knowledge for improving mood and mental health through artistic and architectural practices continues to expand.

"In the architecture of music, we build sanctuaries
for our spirits, designing soundscapes that shelter
us from the storms of life."

❥❥❥

NINETEEN

HARMONIZING HUES: COLOR THEORY IN ARTISTIC THERAPY

Color theory is an essential pillar in the field of artistic therapy, providing insights into how colors can influence mood, emotional responses, and even physiological reactions. This interplay between color and human psychology is crucial for therapists who use art as a means of healing and expression. Understanding color theory allows therapists to guide individuals in using colors to explore and modify their emotions, offering a non-verbal medium through which to express complex feelings and thoughts.

The Basics of Color Theory

Color theory encompasses the relationships and dynamics between colors, explaining how they interact visually and the psychological impact they might have. It involves the color wheel, color harmony, and the context in which colors are used. Primary colors (red, blue, yellow) can be combined to create secondary and tertiary colors, providing a wide spectrum for expression.

Color Psychology in Therapy

In therapeutic settings, colors are used deliberately to evoke or soothe emotions. Red might stimulate feelings of passion and energy but can also increase anxiety or discomfort if overused. Blue, often associated with calmness and serenity, is favored in environments where stress reduction is the goal. Green, reminiscent of nature, promotes relaxation and has been shown to reduce stress. Understanding these effects allows therapists to create art assignments that can help clients express or modulate their emotions effectively.

Using Colors to Explore Emotional States

Art therapists often encourage clients to use specific colors to represent their feelings or emotional states. This exercise can help clients visualize and confront emotions they might find difficult to articulate. For example, asking a client to paint a picture using colors that represent their anxiety can lead to revelations about the emotions underlying their anxiety, fostering a deeper understanding and opening pathways to healing.

Color and Mood Regulation

Colors are not only used to explore and express emotions but also to regulate mood. For instance, incorporating calming colors into an art therapy session can create a soothing atmosphere, potentially making it easier for clients to open up and engage in the therapeutic process. Conversely, vibrant colors might be introduced to energize a client who feels lethargic or depressed.

Healing Through Color Harmony

Color harmony refers to the aesthetically pleasing arrangement of colors, which can enhance balance and visual coherence in an artwork. In therapy, creating harmonious color palettes can be a calming and satisfying experience for clients, providing a sense of accomplishment and aesthetic pleasure, which in itself can be therapeutic. This practice can be particularly beneficial for clients struggling with anxiety or obsessive-compulsive disorders, as it offers a structured and controlled creative outlet.

Cultural Significance of Colors

Art therapists are also mindful of the cultural contexts in which their clients perceive color. Colors can have different meanings in different cultures—a fact that can significantly influence how clients react to certain colors. For instance, while white is often associated with purity and peace in many Western cultures, it might be seen as a color of mourning in some Eastern cultures. Being sensitive to these differences is crucial in a therapeutic setting.

Interactive Use of Color in Therapy

Interactive art therapy sessions that focus on color use can facilitate a deeper engagement with emotions and foster a better understanding of one's mental state. Techniques might include creating mood boards, collages, or mixed media pieces that incorporate various colors to represent different aspects of the client's life or emotional landscape.

Educational and Developmental Benefits

Educational aspects of color theory in artistic therapy include teaching clients how different colors can be mixed to create new hues or how colors can influence each other when placed side by side. This education can empower clients, giving them more control over their artistic expressions and, by extension, their emotional explorations.

Integrating Technology with Color Therapy

Advancements in technology have also influenced how color theory is utilized in therapy. Digital art therapy platforms can offer clients the ability to experiment with colors in a virtual environment, which can be particularly useful for those who are inhibited about using physical paints or those who are exploring art therapy in remote settings.

Color theory plays a vital role in the practice of artistic therapy, serving as a bridge between visual art and psychological healing. By understanding and applying the principles of color theory, therapists can enhance the therapeutic process, helping clients express, explore, and understand their emotions in a profound and impactful way. As clients learn to use colors to communicate their feelings, they often discover new paths to emotional health and personal insight, demonstrating the power of color in the healing arts.

ᐅᐅᐅ

"Art does not change things on its own, but it can inspire those who see it to change the world, one perspective at a time."

♡♡♡

TWENTY

THE CHOREOGRAPHY OF CONNECTION: BUILDING BONDS THROUGH DANCE

Dance, as both an art form and a medium of expression, has a profound capacity to foster human connection and build community. Through its inherent physicality and expressive nature, dance can transcend verbal communication, enabling individuals to communicate emotions, share experiences, and build relationships in ways that words alone cannot achieve. The choreography of connection explored through dance offers a unique and powerful pathway to social cohesion, emotional resonance, and interpersonal understanding.

Dance as a Social Connector

Historically, dance has played a crucial role in social gatherings, rituals, and celebrations across cultures. It acts as a powerful social binder, bringing people together through shared movement and rhythm. In many cultures, dance is a way to celebrate milestones, express communal values, and strengthen bonds within the group. This communal aspect of dance is not just about entertainment; it serves deeper social functions, facilitating a sense of belonging and collective identity.

Therapeutic Benefits of Dance

In therapeutic contexts, dance is used to enhance both physical and emotional well-being. Dance movement therapy (DMT), a recognized therapeutic approach, utilizes dance to support intellectual, emotional, and motor functions of the body. By engaging with dance, individuals can explore emotional expressions and experiences through body movements, which can be particularly beneficial for those who find verbal communication challenging. This form of therapy is used to treat a range of issues, including anxiety, depression, and neurological disorders, fostering emotional healing through physical expression.

Enhancing Emotional Intelligence Through Dance

Dance requires an awareness of one's own body in space, as well as a sensitivity to the movements of others. In a group dance setting, participants must attune to the rhythms and movements of their partners or the group, fostering a non-verbal form of communication and mutual understanding. This process can enhance emotional intelligence, as dancers become more attuned to non-verbal cues such as facial expressions, posture, and gestures, which are key components of emotional communication.

Building Trust and Cooperation

Partner dances, such as tango, salsa, or ballroom dancing, require a high level of cooperation and trust between partners. Dancers must work closely together, often relying on each other to perform complex movements or maintain balance. This dependency builds trust and can be a profound exercise in vulnerability and cooperation, which are foundational aspects of deep personal relationships.

Dance and Community Health

Community dance programs are increasingly recognized for their role in promoting health and well-being at a community level. These programs often target diverse groups, including the elderly, at-risk youth, or culturally diverse populations, offering a space not only for physical activity but also for social interaction and community building. Such initiatives can reduce feelings of isolation, improve mental health, and enhance the overall social fabric of the community.

Overcoming Cultural and Linguistic Barriers

Dance can transcend cultural and linguistic barriers, making it an effective medium for integration and multicultural interaction. In communities with diverse populations, dance can serve as a universal language that facilitates communication and understanding across cultural divides. By participating in dance styles from different cultures, individuals can gain insights into each other's traditions and values, fostering mutual respect and intercultural dialogue.

Dance in Educational Settings

In educational contexts, dance is used to promote not only physical fitness but also social and emotional learning. School dance programs can help students develop teamwork skills, enhance self-esteem, and reduce anxiety. Dance provides students with opportunities to express themselves creatively, work collaboratively in groups, and develop leadership skills, all of which are important for personal and academic success.

Promoting Inclusivity Through Dance

Dance can be particularly empowering for marginalized or disabled individuals, offering a platform for expression and visibility. Inclusive dance companies and programs emphasize the ability of dance to adapt to different bodies and abilities, challenging traditional notions of who can be a dancer and what dance looks like. This inclusivity not only enriches the dance community but also promotes broader societal acceptance and appreciation of diversity.

Documenting and Sharing Dance Experiences

The rise of digital media has allowed for the sharing and documenting of dance across global platforms, expanding the reach and impact of dance as a tool for connection. Online dance challenges, virtual dance classes, and social media platforms have enabled people from all over the world to share their movements and stories, creating virtual communities bound by a love of dance.

Dance serves as a dynamic and multifaceted medium for building connections and fostering community. Whether through structured therapy, community programs, educational initiatives, or informal social dancing, the act of dancing with others can bridge gaps, heal emotional wounds, and bring people together in profound and enduring ways. As society continues to recognize the value of dance in building and sustaining connections, it is likely to remain an essential element in the choreography of human relationships, celebrating the unifying power of movement across diverse cultures and communities.

♭♭♭

"Every color has a voice, every hue an emotion, and
in the palette of the artist lies the power to speak to
souls, guiding them from darkness to light."

ᗊᗊᗊ

TWENTY-ONE

SUMMARY: EXPLORING THE ARTS AS A PATHWAY TO HEALING AND CONNECTION

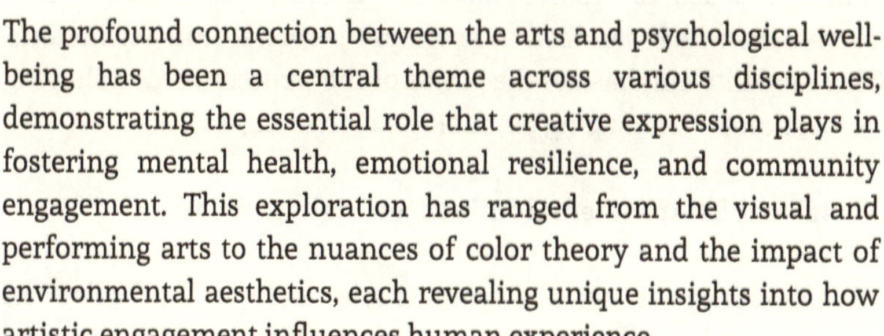

The profound connection between the arts and psychological well-being has been a central theme across various disciplines, demonstrating the essential role that creative expression plays in fostering mental health, emotional resilience, and community engagement. This exploration has ranged from the visual and performing arts to the nuances of color theory and the impact of environmental aesthetics, each revealing unique insights into how artistic engagement influences human experience.

Art Therapy: A Multifaceted Approach

Art therapy has been shown to be a powerful tool for self-expression and emotional exploration. Through different mediums such as painting, sculpture, and drawing, individuals find avenues to express complex feelings and experiences, often leading to significant therapeutic outcomes. These creative processes help articulate thoughts and emotions that are otherwise difficult to express, allowing for cathartic release and emotional healing.

The Healing Rhythms of Music and Dance

Music therapy harnesses the universal language of music to address emotional, cognitive, physical, and social needs. It taps into the inherent musicality of human beings to improve mental health, enhance cognitive functions, and foster social integration. Similarly, dance serves as both an art form and a mode of physical and emotional therapy, promoting connection through movement. It supports emotional and physical well-being by encouraging self-expression, enhancing mood, and building community.

Literary Arts: Writing as Catharsis

Creative writing provides a powerful means for dealing with personal trauma and enhancing personal insight. It offers a cathartic space for individuals to articulate and reshape their narratives, which can lead to profound personal transformations. This modality emphasizes the power of the written word in shaping perception and managing psychological challenges.

Visual and Environmental Influences: Light and Color

The influence of visual stimuli such as light and color on psychological well-being is profound. Lighting in art and architecture significantly affects mood and cognition, shaping how individuals feel within a space. Similarly, color theory in artistic therapy explores how colors can be strategically used to influence emotions and behaviors, enhancing therapeutic settings and promoting mental health.

Building Bonds Through Performance

Performance arts like theater and dance not only entertain but also build deep connections among people, acting as a bridge between diverse cultures and personal experiences. These arts foster community, enhance empathy, and support social interaction, making them vital in therapeutic and educational settings.

The Role of Art in Community and Education

Art extends beyond individual therapy and is a vital component of community building and education. Community art programs and educational initiatives leverage the power of art to foster social cohesion, enhance educational outcomes, and promote inclusive practices. These programs often target various groups, fostering a sense of belonging and community resilience.

Technological Advancements and the Future of Art Therapy

The integration of technology into the arts opens new avenues for therapeutic practices. Digital platforms for music, dance, and visual arts therapy allow for greater accessibility and innovation in treatment methodologies. These technologies offer personalized therapeutic experiences and reach wider audiences, showcasing the adaptability and evolving nature of arts therapy.

Inclusive Practices in Artistic Therapy

Artistic therapy is inherently inclusive, providing platforms for expression that adapt to various needs and abilities. This inclusiveness challenges traditional perceptions of art and therapy, promoting diversity and acceptance within the artistic community and broader society.

The exploration of the arts as a pathway to healing and connection underscores a fundamental truth: the arts are not merely for aesthetic enjoyment but are crucial for mental and emotional well-being. As we continue to navigate the complexities of human psychology, the arts remain a vital tool for healing, teaching, and connecting us in more profound ways. Through continued research, practice, and integration of new technologies, the potential for the arts to foster health and well-being is boundless, promising richer, more empathetic interactions in a world that increasingly recognizes the value of creativity and expression in fostering a healthier society.

ᗡᗡᗡ

Citation And References

This book represents the culmination of extensive research and meticulous analysis, incorporating a diverse range of sources, including numerous books, scholarly studies, and personal experiences. Additionally, I have scoured various websites to gather relevant information and data essential for the compilation of this work. I have taken every precaution to ensure the accuracy of the information presented and have diligently cited all sources to acknowledge their contributions.

Despite these efforts, the possibility of inadvertent errors remains. I deeply value the insights of my readers and appreciate any feedback that can help identify and rectify such inaccuracies. I encourage you to bring any discrepancies to my attention.

Your feedback is not only welcome but crucial, as it will aid in correcting current editions and enhancing the content of future ones. I am committed to maintaining the highest standards of accuracy and reliability in my work and thank you for your support and understanding.

Additionally, I firmly uphold the principle of freedom of speech and expression as guaranteed under Article 19(1)(a) of the Constitution of India, and I respect the diverse viewpoints and expressions of all readers.

ᚦᚦᚦ

Other Books Of The Author

1. Empowering Minds: A Journey into Women's Self-Discovery and Power
2. The Dynamics of Motivation: Catalyzing Thought into Action
3. Meditation and Mental Well Being: The Path to Inner Peace and Clarity
4. The Psychology of Child Education: Nurturing Future Generations
5. Ethical Enlightenment: A Modern Guide to Living with Integrity
6. Voices of Empowerment: Stories of Women Rising Against Odds
7. Social Psychology in Everyday Life: Understanding Human Connections
8. The Essence of Motivational Speaking: Inspiring Change in Others
9. Balancing Acts: Women, Work, and the Will to Lead
10. Guiding with Grace: Raising Children with Compassion and Awareness
11. The Power of Positive Aging: Embracing Life After Fifty
12. Building Resilient Communities: Social Work in Action
13. The Ethical Educator: Principles for Teaching and Learning
14. From Insight to Impact: Social Psychology for a Better World
15. The Ethics of Empathy: A Guide to Ethical Living
16. The Science of Empowering the Self: Navigating Life's Challenges with Psychological Wisdom
17. The Mindful Conscious Leader: Meditation Techniques for Modern Management
18. Pioneering Spirit: Women's Pathways to Leadership and Empowerment
19. Feeling to Healing: The Role of Emotional Intelligence in Child Development
20. Transformative Talks and Words of Inspiration: Insights into Motivational Oratory

Contact

Dr. Minakshi Bansal
Social Activist
Ahmedabad, Gujarat, Bharat
minakshiindiag20@yahoo.com

ᐅᐅᐅ

|| LOKAHA SAMASTHAHA SUKHINO BHAVANTU ||

• 133 •

www.ingramcontent.com/pod-product-compliance
Lightning Source LLC
Chambersburg PA
CBHW020839150726
48196CB00002B/132